This book belongs to: _

You only fail when you stop trying
- unknown

Made in the USA
Columbia, SC
16 July 2025

60793805R00070